Contents

Though high-protein diets are frequently touted for weight loss, some studies point to higher body weights among meat-eaters. While animal proteins contribute to malnutrition, they may also be higher in calories, making it harder to produce the calorie deficit demanded for weight loss. In fact, one study that looked at five- time weight changes among more than adults found that total meat, red meat and poultry consumption were associated with weight gain over the study period, indeed after adjusting for factors such as exercise. The study suggests that consuming about nine ounces of meat per day could contribute to a four-and-a-half pound gain over five years. While this exploration doesn't show that eating beast protein causes weight gain, it does point out a flaw in the thinking that eating meat is a definitive weight- reducing strategy.

Additionally, a 2018 review of almost a dozen studies plant that when compared to typical dietary advice for diabetes, a plant-based diet was tied to better physical and emotional well-being, including better weight-loss outcomes, among actors. Another 2020 review found that, for the most part, transitioning from an feral diet to a plant-based diet was linked to weight loss.

The main idea is to make factory- grounded foods the central part of your refections. " A plant-based diet emphasizes foods like fruits, vegetables, and beans, and limits foods like meats, dairy, and eggs," Manaker says. From there, more restrictions could be put in place depending on how strict you want to be. " It may completely eliminate foods from animals or just limit input, depending on the individual's interpretation," Manaker says.

That means meat and seafood do n't necessarily need to be off-limits — you might just decide to cut down on how constantly you eat those particulars.

Think of " plant-based" as a broad order of diets, with other more specific diets falling under its umbrella. For example, the Mediterranean diet is a version of a plant-based diet because even though it incorporates fish and poultry, the emphasis is on plant-based foods, Manaker says.

Vegetarian and vegan diets are also plant-based. (1) Whole30, a popular diet and life plan, doesn't usually qualify. " The Whole30 diet traditionally is heavier on animal proteins, though it is possible to follow this diet in a plant-based way,"

Plant-Based Diet

A factory- grounded diet is any diet that focuses on shops first. This includes nutrient-dense fruits, vegetables, nuts, seeds, whole grains and legumes. With that said, plant-based doesn't have to mean factory- exclusive. Moderate quantities of meat, poultry, fish, seafood, eggs and dairy can all be included. Simply put, when following a factory- grounded diet you 're choosing to eat more shops.

Plant-based eating may summon a certain kind of imagery rustic grains and bountiful kale, golden turmeric tinctures, earthenware coliseums overflowing with farmers market roughage.

But beyond the romance, what does this kind of eating actually number? For some, it mimics a vegan diet. Others continue to work animal products, like honey or cheese, into the force. While the term has surged in popularity in recent years, it lacks a clear-cut definition. All of the cooks I spoke with seem to agree that " plant-based" connotes more of a holistic lifestyle, rather than an ironclad set of dos and do n'ts.

Variety of Plant-Based Diets
A factory- grounded diet consists of mainly whole, plantbased foods like whole grains, legumes (sap, peas, lentils), vegetables, fruits, seeds, and nuts. There are many different types of plant-based diets and they are categorized grounded on the extent meat is included. Some of the further popular ones include semi-vegetarian or flexitarian, pescatarians, lacto-ovo vertebrate, and insectivores. Here is a summary of vegetarian diets

Semi-vegetarian or flexitarian is someone who is primarily a vegetarian but will also consume small quantities of meat, poultry, fish, and seafood. They also might include dairy foods and eggs. This type of eating is more flexible compared to something like a vegan diet and is a good starting place for individuals looking to incorporate more plant-based refections. Pescatarians are individualities who are primarily vegetarian, but they also will consume shellfish and fish.

Lacto-ovo vegetarian diet is a factory- grounded diet that also includes eggs and dairy products. The diet excludes meat, fish, poultry, and any products that contain these foods.

Vegan diets exclude meat, eggs, and dairy products. Vegans also count all animal-derived ingredients. An important note for insectivores is the importance of vitamin B-12. Vitamin B-12 is plant only in beast foods, some fortified cereals, or some nutritional yeast, so vegans need to take vitamin B-12 as a supplement to ensure acceptable intake.

There are many other plant-based diets that individualities may choose to follow. An important fact for any of these vegetarian eating plans or diets is that they can work for everyone and individuals have the choice of what they want to include or exclude.

What Can You Eat on a Factory- Grounded Diet

When picturing what a plant-based meal looks like, fruits and vegetables presumably come to mind. And they're an important part of just about any healthy diet. But you're not limited to these foods. There are a wide variety of plant foods to enjoy. The major types of food typically eaten on a plant-based diet include

• Fruits — Ex Apples, berries, kiwis, mangoes, avocado, bananas, jackfruit,etc.

• Vegetables — Ex Onions, broccoli, beets, potatoes, mushrooms, carrots, etc.

• Whole grains — Ex Quinoa, millet, buckwheat, wheat, rice, corn, etc.

• Sap & legumes — Ex Black beans, chickpeas, lentils, edamame, peas, etc.

• Nuts & seeds — Ex Almonds, cashews, chia seeds, flaxseeds, walnuts,etc.

• Sauces & spices — Ex Turmeric, ginger, cinnamon, oregano, garlic, cayenne,etc.

• Fermented foods — Ex Kimchi, sauerkraut, miso, natto, etc.

Eating across all these food groups will help you get an cornucopia of micronutrients from your food. Also, when choosing from each category, suppose " eat the rainbow." Various factory foods are full of phytochemicals (a fancy word that just means " chemicals from shops) and antioxidants that are good for keeping different parts of your body healthy.

How to start a plant grounded diet for beginners

Are you ready to get started? Unveiling, our most comprehensive list yet how to start a factory based diet for beginners! Then's what to do

Review the recipes, listed by type. A plant based foods list is overwhelming. Then we 've systematized our recipes by type. Plant grounded eating revolves around main types of recipes based on function, from soups to sandwiches to tacos to breakfasts to snacks.

Remember plant based protein. Most of the recipes below are loaded with plant based protein. Review the list above, and if necessary serve with a side that includes it. A side salad with nuts and seeds or even a sprinkle of almonds works.

Pick one and start! If you 're looking to start a factory based diet, you do n't have to know everything before you get started. Just pick one form and make it! If you like it, great! Save that for thefuture.However, move on and keep trying things until you develop your tastes, If not.

How do I get protein

Factory based foods are any foods that contain no beast products (meat, dairy, eggs, honey). Then's the most important part of plant based eating protein is key for staying satiated and full. Alex and I have been doing this plant grounded eating thing for years. And we've learned the most important part of eating vegan and vegetarian fashions is to make sure they're packed withprotein.However, we 'll be empty an hour later, If not. Luckily, there lots of options for adding plant grounded protein to your meals to make them filling and nutritious. Here's a factory grounded food list with the top protein-filled foods

• Legumes Try lentils (red, green, brown, French), split peas, black-eyed peas, and beans (black, garbanzo/ chickpeas, lima, navy, pinto, white, and kidney)

• Grains Try quinoa, barley, bulgur wheat, amaranth, millet, and brown and wild rice (see How to Cook Whole Grains)

• Nuts and seeds Try almonds, cashews, peanuts, walnuts, pecans, hazelnuts, pistachios, pumpkin seeds, sesame seeds, sunflower seeds

• Soy Soy based products like tofu and tempeh are rich in plant based protein; stick to 2 to 4 servings per week.

• Veggies Some vegetables have protein, but in much

lower amounts than the foods over. Some higher protein veggies are corn, broccoli, asparagus, Brussels sprouts, and artichokes.

When you're eating lots of protein from plants, it's important to get a wide variety of protein sources.

Healthy Weight

When it comes to weight loss, there's no lack of fad diets promising fast results. But such diets limit your nutritive input, can be unhealthy, and tend to fail in the long run.

The crucial to achieving and maintaining a healthy weight is n't about short- term salutary changes. It's about a life that includes healthy eating, regular physical exertion, and balancing the number of calories you consume with the number of calories your body uses. Staying in control of your weight contributes to good health now and as you age

How numerous calories are used in typical conditioning

Regular physical activity is important for good health, and it's especially important if you're trying to lose weight or to maintain a healthy weight.

When losing weight, more physical activity increases the number of calories your body uses for energy or " burns off." The burning of calories through physical activity, combined with reducing the number of calories you eat, creates a " calorie deficit" that results in weight loss. Most weight loss occurs because of decreased sweet intake. However, evidence shows the only way to maintain weight loss is to be engaged in regular physical exertion.

Most importantly, physical exertion reduces risks of cardiovascular complaint and diabetes beyond that produced by weight reduction alone. Physical activity also helps to –

• Maintain weight.

• Reduce high blood pressure.

• Reduce risk for type 2 diabetes, heart attack, stroke,

and several forms of cancer.

• Reduce arthritis pain and associated disability.

• Reduce risk for osteoporosis and falls.

• Reduce symptoms of depression and anxiety.

How much physical activity do I need

When it comes to weight operation, people vary greatly in how much physical activity they need. Here are some guidelines to follow

• To maintain your weight Work your way up to 150 twinkles of moderate-intensity aerobic exertion, 75 minutes of vigorous-intensity aerobic exertion, or an equivalent blend of the two each week. Strong scientific evidence shows that physical activity can help you maintain your weight over time. However, the exact amount of physical exertion demanded to do this is not clear since it varies greatly from person to person. It's possible that you may need to do further than the equivalent of 150 minutes of moderate- intensity exertion a week to maintain your weight.

• To lose weight and keep it off You will need a high amount of physical exertion unless you also adjust your diet and reduce the amount of calories you 're eating and drinking. Getting to and staying at a healthy weight requires both regular physical activity and a healthy eating plan.

What do moderate and vigorous-intensity mean
• Moderate While performing the physical exertion, if your breathing and heart rate is noticeably faster but you can still carry on a conversation — it's probably moderately violent. Exemplifications include —
• Walking briskly (a 15- nanosecond mile).
• Light yard work (raking/ bagging leaves or using a lawn mower).
• Light snow shoveling.
• Actively playing with children.
• Biking at a casual pace.

• Vigorous Your heart rate is increased substantially and

you are breathing too hard and fast to have a discussion, it's probably roundly violent. Examples include —

• Jogging/ running.

• Swimming laps.

• Rollerblading/ inline skating at a brisk pace.

• Cross-country skiing.

• Utmost competitive sports (football, basketball, or soccer).

• Jumping rope.

How to Lose Weight and Keep It Off

What's the best diet for healthy weight loss

Pick up any diet book and it will claim to hold all the answers to successfully losing all the weight you want — and keeping it off. Some claim the key is to eat less and exercise more, others that low fat is the only way to go, while others prescribe cutting out carbs. So, what should you believe?

The verity is there is no " one size fits all" result to

permanent healthy weight loss. What works for one person may not work for you, since our bodies respond else to different foods, depending on genetics and other health factors. To find the method of weight loss that's right for you will likely take time and require patience, commitment, and some experimentation with different foods and diets.

While some people respond well to counting calories or similar restrictive styles, others respond better to having more freedom in planning their weight-loss programs. Being free to simply avoid fried foods or cut back on refined carbs can set them up for success. So, don't get too discouraged if a diet that worked for somebody else does n't work for you. And don't beat yourself up if a diet proves too restrictive for you to stick with. Ultimately, a diet is only right for you if it's one you can stick with over time.

Remember while there's no easy fix to losing weight, there are plenty of way you can take to develop a healthier relationship with food, curb emotional triggers to gluttony, and achieve a healthy weight.

Weight loss strategies

1. Cut calories

Some experts believe that successfully managing your weight comes down to a simple equation If you eat smaller calories than you burn, you lose weight. Sounds readily, right? Then why is losing weight so hard? Weight loss is n't a linear event over time. When you cut calories, you may drop weight for the first few weeks, for example, and also something changes. You eat the same number of calories but you lose lower weight or no weight at all. That's because when you lose weight you 're losing water and spare tissue as well as fat, your metabolism slows, and your body changes in other ways. So, in order to continue dropping weight each week, you need to continue cutting calories.

A calorie isn't always a calorie. Eating 100 calories of high fructose corn syrup, for example, can have a different effect on your body than eating 100 calories of broccoli. The trick for sustained weight loss is to ditch the foods that are packed with calories but don't make you feel full (like candy) and replace them with foods that fill you up without being loaded with calories (like vegetables).

Many of us do n't always eat simply to satisfy hunger. We also turn to food for comfort or to relieve stress — which can quickly derail any weight loss plan.

2. Cut carbs

A different way of viewing weight loss identifies the problem as not one of consuming too many calories, but rather the way the body accumulates fat after consuming carbohydrates — in particular the role of the hormone insulin. When you eat a meal, carbohydrates from the food enter your bloodstream as glucose. In order to keep your blood sugar levels in check, your body always burns off this glucose before it burns off fat from a meal.

Still, rice, chuck, If you eat a carbohydrate-rich meal (

lots of pasta. As well as regulating blood sugar levels, insulin does two effects It prevents your fat cells from releasing fat for the body to burn as energy (because its priority is to burn off the glucose) and it creates more fat cells for storing everything that your body ca n't burn off. The result is that you gain weight and your body now requires more fuel to burn, so you eat more. Since insulin only burns carbohydrates, you crave carbs and so begins a vicious cycle of consuming carbs and gaining weight. To lose weight, the reasoning goes, you need to break this cycle by reducing carbs.

Most low-carb diets advocate replacing carbs with protein and fat, which could have some negative long-term goods on yourhealth.However, you can reduce your pitfalls and limit your intake of impregnated and trans fats by choosing spare meats, fish and vegetarian sources of protein, If you do try a low-carb diet.

3. Cut fat

It's a mainstay of many diets if you don't want to get fat, don't eat fat. Walk down any grocery store aisle and you 'll be bombarded with reduced-fat snacks, dairy, and packaged meals. But while our low-fat options have exploded, so have obesity rates. So, why haven't low-fat diets worked for more of us?

Not all fat is bad. Healthy or " good" fats can actually help to control your weight, as well as manage your moods and fight fatigue. Unsaturated fats plant in avocados, nuts, seeds, soy milk, tofu, and fatty fish can help fill you over, while adding a little tasty olive oil to a plate of vegetables, for example, can make it easier to eat healthy food and improve the overall quality of your diet.

We often make the wrong trade-offs. Many of us make the mistake of swapping fat for the empty calories of sugar and meliorated carbohydrates. Instead of eating whole-fat yoghurt, for example, we eat low-or no-fat versions that are packed with sugar to make up for the loss of taste. Or we exchange our fatty breakfast bacon for a muffin or donut that causes rapid spikes in blood sugar.

4. Follow the Mediterranean diet

The Mediterranean diet emphasizes eating good fats and good carbs along with large quantities of fresh fruits and vegetables, nuts, fish, and olive canvas — and only modest amounts of meat and cheese. The Mediterranean diet is further than just about food, though. Regular physical activity and participating refections with others are also major factors. Whatever weight loss strategy you try, it's important to stay motivated and avoid common dieting risks, such as emotional eating.

Control emotional eating

We do n't always eat simply to satisfy hunger. All too frequently, we turn to food when we 're stressed-out or anxious, which can wreck any diet and pack on the pounds. Do you eat when you're worried, bored, or lonely? Do you snack in front of the TV at the end of a stressful day? Feting your emotional eating triggers can make all the difference in your weight- loss efforts. If you eat when you 're

• Stressed – find healthier ways to calm yourself. Try yoga, meditation, or soaking in a hot bath.

• Low on energy – find other mid-afternoon pick-me-ups. Try walking around the block, harkening to energizing music, or taking a short nap.

• Lonely or bored – reach out to others rather of reaching for the refrigerator. Call a friend who makes you laugh, take your dog for a walk, or go to the library, mall, or park — anywhere there's people.

• Practice mindful eating rather

• Avoid distractions while eating. Try not to eat while working, watching Television, or driving. It's too easy to mindlessly gormandize.

• Pay attention. Eat slowly, savoring the smells and textures of yourfood.However, gently return your attention to your food and how it tastes, If your mind wanders.

• Mix things up to focus on the experience of eating. Try

using chopsticks rather than a fork, or use your utensils with your non-dominant hand.

• Stop eating before you are full. It takes time for the signal to reach your brain that you 've had enough. Do n't feel indebted to always clean your plate.

Stay motivated

Endless weight loss requires making healthy changes to your lifestyle and food choices. To stay motivated

• Find a cheering section. Social support means a lot. Programs like Jenny Craig and Weight Watchers use group support to impact weight loss and lifelong healthy eating. Seek out support — whether in the form of family, friends, or a support group — to get the encouragement you need.

• Slow and steady wins the race. Losing weight too fast can take a risk on your mind and body, making you feel sluggish, drained, and sick. Aim to lose one to two pounds a week so you 're losing fat rather than water and muscle.

• Set goals to keep you motivated. Short-term pretensions, like wanting to fit into a bikini for the summer, usually don't work as well as wanting to feel more confident or become healthier for your children's sakes. When temptation strikes, focus on the benefits you 'll reap from being healthier.

• Use tools to track your progress. Smartphone apps, fitness trackers, or simply keeping a journal can help you keep track of the food you eat, the calories you burn, and the weight you lose. Seeing the results in black and white can help you stay motivated.

• Get plenty of sleep. Lack of sleep stimulates your appetite so you want more food than normal; at the same time, it stops you feeling satisfied, making you want to keep eating. Sleep deprivation can also affect your motivation, so end for eight hours of quality sleep a night.

Cut down on sugar and refined carbs

Whether or not you're specifically aiming to cut carbs, utmost of us consume unhealthy amounts of sugar and meliorated carbohydrates such as white bread, pizza dough, pasta, pastries, white flour, white rice, and candied breakfast cereals. Replacing meliorated carbs with their whole-grain counterparts and eliminating delicacy and goodies is only part of the result, though. Sugar is hidden in foods as diverse as canned soups and vegetables, pasta sauce, margarine, and many reduced fat foods. Since your body gets each it needs from sugar naturally occurring in food, all this added sugar amounts to nothing but a lot of empty calories and unhealthy spikes in your blood glucose.

Lower sugar can mean a slimmer waistline
Calories attained from fructose (found in sticky beverages such as soda and reused foods like doughnuts, muffins, and delicacy) are more likely to add to fat around your belly. Cutting back on sugary foods can mean a slimmer waistline as well as a lower risk of

diabetes.

Fill up with fruit, veggies, and fiber

Even if you're cutting calories, that doesn't inescapably mean you have to eat lower food. High-fiber foods such as fruit, vegetables, beans, and whole grains are higher in volume and take longer to digest, making them filling — and great for weight-loss.

It's generally okay to eat as important fresh fruit andnon-starchy vegetables as you want — you 'll feel full before you 've overdone it on the calories.

• Eat vegetables raw or steamed, not fried or breaded, and dress them with herbs and spices or a little olive canvas for flavor.

• Add fruit to low sugar cereal — blueberries, strawberries, sliced bananas. You 'll still enjoy lots of sweetness, but with fewer calories, less sugar, and further fiber.

• Bulk out sandwiches by adding healthy veggie choices like lettuce, tomatoes, sprouts, cucumbers, and avocado.

• Snack on carrots or celery with hummus rather of a high-calorie chips and dip.

• Add more veggies to your favorite main courses to make your dish more substantial. Even pasta and stir-feasts can be diet-friendly if you use less noodles and more vegetables.

• Start your meal with salad or vegetable soup to help fill you up so you eat lower of your entrée.

Take charge of your food environment
Set yourself up for weight-loss success by taking charge of your food terrain when you eat, how much you eat, and what foods you make easily available.

• Cook your own refections at home. This allows you to control both portion size and what goes in to the food. Restaurant and packaged foods generally contain a lot more sugar, unhealthy fat, and calories than food cooked at home — plus the portion sizes tend to be larger.

• Serve yourself smaller portions. Use small plates, bowls, and mugs to make your portions appear larger.

Don't eat out of large bowls or directly from food containers, which makes it delicate to assess how much you've eaten.

• Eat early. Studies suggest that consuming more of your daily calories at breakfast and fewer at dinner can help you drop more pounds. Eating a larger, healthy breakfast can jump start your metabolism, stop you feeling empty during the day, and give you more time to burn off the calories.

• Fast for 14 hours a day. Try to eat regale earlier in the day and then fast until breakfast the coming morning. Eating only when you're most active and giving your digestion a long break may aid weight loss.

• Plan your meals and snacks ahead of time. You can produce your own small portion snacks in plastic bags or containers. Eating on a schedule will help you avoid eating when you aren't truly hungry.

• Drink more water. Thirst can frequently be confused with hunger, so by drinking water you can avoid extra calories.

• Limit the amount of tempting foods you have athome.However, store indulgent foods out of sight, If you share a kitchen withnon-dieters.

Get moving

The degree to which exercise aids weight loss is open to debate, but the benefits go way beyond burning calories. Exercise can increase your metabolism and ameliorate your outlook — and it's something you can benefit from right now. Go for a walk, stretch, move around and you 'll have more energy and provocation to attack the other steps in your weight-loss program.

• Lack time for a long drill? Three 10- nanosecond spurts of exercise per day can be just as good as one 30-nanosecond workout.

• Remember anything is better than nothing. Start off sluggishly with small amounts of physical exertion each day. Then, as you start to lose weight and have more energy, you 'll find it easier to become more physically active.

• Find exercise you enjoy. Try walking with a friend, dancing, hiking, cycling, playing Frisbee with a canine, enjoying a pickup game of basketball, or playing activity-based video games with your kiddies.

Keeping the Weight Off

You may have heard the widely quoted statistic that 95 of people who lose weight on a diet will regain it within a few times or even months. While there isn't much hard evidence to support that claim, it is true that many weight- loss plans fail in the long term. Often that's simply because diets that are too restrictive are very hard to maintain over time. However, that doesn't mean your weight loss attempts are doomed to failure. Far from it.

Since it was established in 1994, The National Weight Control Registry (NWCR) in the United States, has tracked over individualities who have lost significant amounts of weight and kept it off for long periods of time. The study has plant that participants who've been successful in maintaining their weight loss share some common strategies. Whatever diet you use to lose weight in the first place.

Adopting these habits may help you to keep it off

• Stay physically active. Successful dieters in the NWCR study exercise for about 60 minutes, typically walking.

• Keep a food log. Recording what you eat every day helps to keep you accountable and motivated.

• Eat breakfast every day. Most commonly in the study, it's cereal and fruit. Eating breakfast boosts metabolism and staves off hunger later in the day.

• Eat more fiber and less unhealthy fat than the typical American diet.

• Regularly check the scale. Weighing yourself daily may help you to detect any small gains in weight, enabling you to promptly take corrective action before the problem escalates.

• Watch less TV. Cutting back on the time spent sitting in front of a screen can be a key part of adopting a more active lifestyle and precluding weight gain.

Nutrients of particular interest in factory- grounded

diets

As described above, plant-based diets have been shown to convey nutritional benefits, in particular increased fiber, beta carotene, vitamin K and C, folate, magnesium, and potassium input and an improved dietary health index83. However, a major criticism of plant-based diets is the risk of nutrient deficiencies for specific micronutrients, especially vitamin B12, a substantially beast- deduced nutrient, which is missing entirely in vegan diets unless supplemented or provided in B12- fortified products, and which seems detrimental for neurological and cognitive health when input is low. In the EPIC-Oxford study about 50 of the vegan dieters showed serum situations indicating vitamin B12 deficiency. Along other threat factors such as age, diet, and plant-based diets in particular, seem to be the main risk factor for vitamin B12 insufficiency, and therefore supplementing vitamin B12 for these threat groups is largely recommended. Vitamin B12 is a pivotal component involved in early brain development, in maintaining normal central nervous system function88 and suggested to be neuroprotective, particularly for memory performance and hippocampal microstructure. One hypothesis is that high levels of homocysteine, that is associated with vitamin B12 deficiency, might be harmful to the body. Vitamin B12 is the essential cofactor needed for the conversion of homocysteine into nonharmful components and serves as a cofactor in different enzymatic reactions. A person suffering from vitamin B12 insufficiency accumulates homocysteine, lastly promoting the formation of plaques in highways and thereby increasing atherothrombotic threat, possibly easing symptoms in patients of Alzheimer's complaint. A meta-analysis found that vitamin B12 insufficiency was associated with stroke, Alzheimer's complaint, vascular madness, Parkinson's disease and in even lower concentrations with cognitive impairment, supporting the claim of its high eventuality for complaint forestallment when avoided or treated. Farther investigations and longitudinal studies are demanded, possibly measuring holotranscobalamin (the active form of vitamin B12) as a more specific and sensitive marker for vitamin B12 status, to examine in how far nonsupplementing vegan dieters could be at risk for cardiovascular and cognitive impairment. Similar health troubles can stem from iron deficiency, another generally assumed risk for factory- grounded dieters and other risk groups such as young women. A meta-analysis on 24 studies proposes that although serum ferritin levels were lower in insectivores on average, it is recommended to sustain an optimal ferritin position (neither too low nor too high), calling for well-monitored supplementation strategies. Iron deficiency is not only dependent on iron input as similar but also on complimentary dietary factors impacting its bioavailability. The picture remains complex on the one hand iron deficiency may lead to mischievous health goods, such as impairments in early brain development and cognitive functions in adults and in children carried by iron-deficient maters and a possible role for iron overload in the brain on cognitive impairment on the other hand. One study showed that attention, memory and learning were impaired in iron-deficient compared to iron-sufficient women, which could be restored after a 4-month oral iron supplementation (n = 118). Iron insufficiency- related impairments could be attributed to anemia as an underlying cause, possibly leading to fatigue, or an undersupply of blood to the brain or differences in neurobiological and neuronal systems provoking impaired cognitive functioning.

This leads to the general recommendation to examiner health status by frequent blood tests, to consult a dietician to live healthily on a factory- grounded diet and to consider supplements to avoid nutrient scarcities or nutrient-overdose-related toxin. All in all, associations similar as the Academy of Nutrition and Dietetics and the German Nutrition Society do not judge iron as a major threat factor for plant-based dieters.

How to Use Fruits and Vegetables to Help Manage Your

Weight

Fruits and vegetables are part of a well-balanced and healthy eating plan. There are many different ways to lose or maintain a healthy weight. Using more fruits and vegetables along with whole grains and lean meats, nuts, and sap is a safe and healthy bone. Helping control your weight is not the only benefit of eating more fruits and vegetables. Diets rich in fruits and vegetables may reduce the threat of some types of cancer and other chronic conditions. Fruits and vegetables also provide essential vitamins and minerals, fiber, and other substances that are important for good health.

To lose weight, you must eat fewer calories than your body uses

This does n't inescapably mean that you have to eat lower food. You can create lower-calorie versions of some of your favorite dishes by substituting low-calorie fruits and vegetables in place of higher-calorie ingredients. The water and fiber in fruits and vegetables will add volume to your dishes, so you can eat the same amount of food with fewer calories. Utmost fruits and vegetables are naturally low in fat and calories and are filling.

Simple ways to cut calories and eat fruits and vegetables throughout your day
Breakfast Start the Day Right
Substitute some spinach, onions, or mushrooms for one of the eggs or half of the rubbish in your morning omelet. The vegetables will add volume and flavor to the dish with smaller calories than the egg or rubbish. Cut back on the amount of cereal in your coliseum to make room for some cut-up bananas, peaches, or strawberries. You can still eat a full bowl, but with fewer calories.
Lighten Up Your Lunch
Substitute vegetables such as lettuce, tomatoes, cucumbers, or onions for 2 ounces of the cheese and 2 ounces of the meat in your sandwich, serape, or burrito. The new interpretation will fill you up with fewer

calories than the original.

Replace 2 ounces of meat or 1 cup of polls in broth-based soup with 1 cup of chopped vegetables, such as broccoli, carrots, beans, or red peppers. The vegetables will help fill you up, so you won't miss those redundant calories.

Dinner

Add in 1 mug of chopped vegetables such as broccoli, tomatoes, squash, onions, or peppers, while removing 1 mug of the rice or pasta in your favorite dish. The dish with the vegetables will be just as satisfying but have fewer calories than the same amount of the original interpretation.

Take a good look at your dinner plate. Vegetables, fruit, and whole grains should take up the largest portion of yourplate.However, replace some of the meat, rubbish, If they do not. This will reduce the total calories in your mess without reducing the amount of food you eat. BUT remember to use a normal-or small-size plate — not a platter. The total number of calories that you eat counts, even if a good proportion of them come from fruits and vegetables.

Plant- grounded weight loss plate

Vegetables

Eat lots of nonstarchy vegetables like leafy greens (lettuce, spinach, kale), broccoli, peppers, cucumbers, jicama, carrots, eggplant, radishes, green beans, onions, and more. PerDr. Joel Fuhrman's guidelines in Eat to Live, 2 pounds of vegetables a day is a great target, but even 1 pound would be awesome. Lush flora are especially good, as they can lower risk of chronic disease.6 And an analysis of further than 200 studies plant that raw vegetables lead the pack when it comes to cancer-fighting potential.7

Fruits

Eat as important as you can in a rainbow of colors! Berries are especially great, as they 're lower in sugar and packed with disease-fighting anthocyanins.

Healthy carbs

Include whole grains like oatmeal, quinoa, millet, wheat berries, and buckwheat. Also have starchy vegetables like potatoes, sweet potatoes, cassava, butternut squash, and pumpkin.

Factory- grounded proteins

All whole factory foods have some protein (even fruit!), but sap, lentils and peas are especially rich sources. Tofu, veggie burgers, and low-fat meat substitutes are great too.

Nuts and seeds

Nuts and seeds are a healthy source of the essential fats your body needs. For most people, a good goal is 1 small sprinkle (1 oz) of nuts and 1 Tbsp of ground flax seed per day.

Water or plant-based milk

Be sure to drink plenty of fluid each day, as thirst can be

mistaken for hunger. Staying doused can also help you think more clearly and improve your mood.9 While plant-based foods do contain ample calcium, plant-based milks can help you get indeed more. Just pick unsweetened,non-coconut varieties of plant milk like almond, soy or cashew.

Vitamin B12
Take vitamin B12 as part of a diurnal multivitamin, or twice a week as a separate supplement.

Best Vegetables to Eat When You're Trying to Lose Weight
Veggies tend to be weight-loss friendly. Why? Most are low in calories and all offer filling fiber, which helps to drift you over and drop those urges to snack. Plus,"the water content of vegetables increases the volume of the food,"says Shahzadi Devje, RD, CDE, MSc, a pukka diabetes educator in Toronto. This helps to keep you

fuller for longer. But some are indeed better than others.

Vegetables that are particularly helpful for weight loss

Spinach

"It's lower in calories, packs a nutritive punch and is versatile to use in all feathers of recipes,"says Devje. Like other leafy flora, spinach is considered a powerhouse vegetable, per a report by theU.S. Centers for Disease Control and Prevention that says it's strongly associated with a reduced risk of habitual conditions — including type 2 diabetes, heart disease, and some types of cancers. Enjoy spinach in a healthy green smoothie, in a lupini bean salad or in a Mason- jar salad.

Broccoli

"This is one of my favorite vegetables for its versatility,"says Marisa Moore, MBA, RDN, a culinary dietitian in Atlanta."It's also a great way to get in some redundant fiber. I like to roast broccoli that's tossed with extra-virgin olive oil and spices. I will eat it as a side dish or make it part of a main by adding it to pasta."Cook up roasted cauliflower and broccoli, a healthy broccoli slaw or beef with broccoli.

Spaghetti squash

Enjoy this winter squash any time you can get your hands on it."It serves as an ideal low-calorie volition to conventional spaghetti. A cup of the cooked squash contains just 42 calories, per the USDA Nutrient Database."It's also low in fat and provides fiber to help you stay full for longer. Add the veggie to funk spaghetti squash, marinara spaghetti squash or chickpea kale curry stuffed spaghetti squash.

Brussels sprouts

"These cruciferous vegetables are loaded with fiber to help you feel full fast and stay satiated for a while."They are very low in calories but have the ability to make you feel less hungry after eating them."A cup of Brussels sprouts has just 38 calories, per the USDA National Nutrient Database. Whip up grilled Brussels sprouts, Brussels sprouts with grape honey glaze or sauteed tattered Brussels sprouts.

Green peas

"With nearly 9 grams of fiber per cup, green peas can help you meet your fiber goals and feel full with ease."I usually keep firmed green peas on hand to add bright green color to soups, puree into a pea pesto, or simply enjoy as a side dressed with olive oil, lemon, swab and pepper."You can also add the green gems to green pea soup, healthy farro fried rice or green peas and mushrooms.

Cauliflower

This veggie contains just 27 calories per cup, per the USDA National Nutrient Database."It provides fiber, which helps to slow digestion and promote a feeling of fullness."Cauliflower is also fat-free, cholesterol-free and low in sodium."Whip up some healthy cauliflower rice, cauliflower tacos or carrot cauliflower soup.

Sweet potato

"With a bit more fiber than white potatoes, sweet potatoes have a satisfying sweet flavor that plays well with foods like kale and black beans."My favorite way to enjoy sweet potatoes is to simply roast them, with the skin on."After all, the skin is where a good amount of the veggie's stuffing fiber sits. Cook up baked sweet potato feasts, sweet potato crust pizza or sweet potato beet hash.

What Do You Avoid on a Plant-Based Diet
When choosing to eat a factory- grounded diet, you 'll want to focus substantially on fresh foods. In a grocery store, that means primarily shopping the outeraisles.However, choose organic foods as much as possible to avoid exposure to GMOs and pesticides, If possible.

Main foods you should avoid on a plant-based diet

• Most or all animal products (Especially factory-farmed meat, eggs, & dairy products)

• Refined sugars (White sugar, club sugar, high fructose sludge syrup, chemical-based calorie-free sweeteners, etc.)

• Largely processed vegetable oils (Corn oil, cottonseed oil, sunflower oil, peanut canvas, soybean canvas, etc.)

• White flour (Especially bleached white flour which is full of chemicals and heavy metals — and nearly devoid of nutrition)

• Junk food (Including most cookies, chips, crackers, snack bars, sweetened drinks, packaged foods, etc.)

• GMOs (The primary genetically engineered crops are sludge, soy, canola, sugar beets, cotton, and alfalfa — plus a bit of apple, zucchini, and potato)

You 'll also want to pay special attention to nutrition labels. By reading labels, you can avoid ultra-processed and dangerous constituents. Packaged foods should have as many constituents as possible. As a general rule,

if you can't pronounce an ingredient, or don't know
what it is, put the food back.

Many packaged foods are full of health claims like "
each-natural" or " non-GMO." But most of these
phrases are branding tactics meant to mislead
consumers into allowing a product is healthy. This is
called " greenwashing."

What Does Plant-Based Eating Look Like Every Day

So, how do these principles translate into real life on a
day-to- day basis? For Wright, a typical day of eating
might number a warm whole-grain porridge with fruit or
a smoothie loaded with flora and healthy fats; grains
and greens drizzled in a homemade sauce or dressing
for lunch; and big salads loaded with grilled veggies, or
perhaps a lentil- grounded pasta tossed with produce
for regale.

" It's very vegetable-forward. " The whole day, I 'm
trying to work fruits or vegetables into every mess,
while grains and nuts are the supporting part."

While the phrase, and how it manifests, may look slightly different to everyone, the consensus seems to be that " plant-based" isn't just about not eating meat or trying to consume a predetermined quantum of yield per day — it's about celebrating shops, rather than relegating them to a side dish or accelerating them with meat substitutes, and doing so with integrity.

For some cooks, that means an occasion to challenge yourself, too. McKinnon says that, for her, working from a more limited span of constituents ultimately yields more creative results. " You have to work harder to create certain flavors and textures, but the prices, I think, are far greater."

What is the difference between plant-based and vegan diets

A vegan diet is the most restrictive of factory- grounded diets. This diet is built around fruits, vegetables, whole grains, legumes, nuts and seeds. Still, unlike other plant-based eating plans, the vegan diet contains zero animal-sourced ingredients. That means no meat, poultry, fish, dairy, eggs or honey.

People come vegan for many reasons – for the welfare of animals, the preservation of the earth, their own personal health and more. Science suggests that vegan diets are more environmentally sustainable than diets rich in animal products and associated with certain health benefits. With that said, for those true meat lovers, the good news is you don't have to banish your favorite foods to reap the health and environmental benefits of plant-based eating.

Why should you consider a plant-based diet

Whole food plant-based diets, filled with produce, whole grains and plant proteins (i.e. nuts, legumes), have been linked to a variety of benefits.

They give essential vitamins and minerals, nourishing fiber and fats, as well as beneficial plant nutrients, which all contribute to overall well-being. Several studies have shown that plant-based eating patterns support a variety of health outcomes, including a healthy heart and healthy weight.

But, that's not all! Picking plants as the star of your meals and snacks isn't only good for you – it's good for the planet too. In fact, according to the 2015 Dietary Guidelines Advisory Committee Report, a diet advanced in plants and lower in beast- grounded foods is associated with less of an impact on the terrain than the typical American diet. In addition, a recent modeling study plant that a healthy vegetarian diet may have a 42 to 84 percent lower burden on the terrain than other salutary patterns. Incipiently, a new report from the EAT-Lancet Commission on Food, Planet and Health further supports the link between diet and environment, calling for a global shift to predominately factory- grounded dietary patterns to ameliorate health and sustainability outcomes.

Plant-based diets and vitamins
Whole food, plant based diets may be the optimal diet to ward off certain cancers, diabetes and rotundity

versus a standard'western diet'. However, vegetarians and especially vegans may need a little more planning when it comes to getting enough of the following minerals and vitamins iron, calcium, selenium, vitamin D, vitamin B12, and omega – 3 and omega-6 fatty acids.

Vitamin B12 – an essential vitamin for the metabolism of every cell in the human body, it is involved in the production of red blood cells and whim-whams cells. B12 is plant only in animal products and is absent from factory- grounded foods, unless they've been fortified. Plant grounded products such as; soy-milk, some breakfast cereals and some meat analogues can be fortified, always check the packaging. The amount of B12 each person needs depends on age and it may be necessary to condense your diet with an oral B12 supplement, if recommended by your doctor or dietician.

Selenium – another essential mineral which cannot be produced by our bodies, selenium plays an important part as part of our immune system and is an antioxidant in low doses. This means it can protect our bodies against free radicals (foreign bodies caused by external sources such as smoking, pollution that can cause our bodies damage). Selenium is usually plant in animal based products similar as meats, eggs, and fish. The best sources within plant based foods are brazil nuts, sunflower seeds, brown rice and beans. As little as two brazil nuts per day will provide you with your quota for the day.

Calcium-is needed for strong bones and teeth but it is also used in numerous other areas of the body, for example blood clotting and muscle compression. Food sources include dairy products, soy, collard flora, broccoli and tofu. Plant based sources of calcium may be less bioavailable than dairy grounded products due to two compounds known as oxalate and phytate found within the factory. These inhibit calcium immersion within the body. So insure you're getting ample calcium through fortified products where you can or supplement if needed. Especially true for vegan diets, or veggie diets which also count dairy.

Iron – plays a vital role in immune system function, transporting oxygen around our bodies through our bloodstream via our haemoglobin and contributing to normal energy situations.

Plant based foods contain a type of iron known as non-heme iron. This type of iron is less fluently absorbed (bioavailable) to us compared to the iron found in animal grounded products known as brim-iron. This is due to the fact the non-heme iron must suffer an extra chemical conversion within our bodies to make it absorbable.

Vitamin C helps or bodies to absorb this type of iron so try to pair factory based sources of iron with a source of vitamin C when planning your meals. Factory based sources of iron include lentils, tofu, chickpeas, sap, chia seeds, ground linseed, hemp seeds, pumpkin seeds, kale, dried apricots, dried figs, raisins and quinoa. Try to brace these with vitamin C containing foods similar as broccoli and citrus fruits to boost the bioavailability of iron. Else, if you are just reducing your meat consumption try to pick animal based products with higher iron levels on the days you do choose to have meat. For example beef, chicken, canned sardines, or tuna.

Vitamin D – this vitamin is demanded for the immersion of calcium into our bodies, thus contributing to the development of strong bones. Our bodies produce Vitamin D when exposed to sunlight. In the UK and Ireland during the winter months it is necessary to get Vitamin D from your diet. Foods such as fatty fish like tuna, mackerel and salmon provide vitamin D. If you are following a factory grounded diet which excludes fish it will be necessary to supplement with vitaminD. Speak to your doctor, dietician or nutritionist about the best supplement for your needs.

Essential Fatty Acids (Omega-3 and Omega-6) – fat is an essential macronutrient which is used by the body as an energy source and helps the body to absorb certain minerals A, D, E andK.

There are two types of essential fats that we need which the body cannot make itself. These are the Omega-3 (alpha-linoleic acid), which is linked to the forestallment of diabetes and some cancersand Om ega-6 (linoleic acid) fatty acids.

Sources of omega-6 (LA) include hemp seeds, sunflower seeds, walnuts and soy spread products. If you are eating a different range of foods whilst following a plant based diet you will be getting enough of this in your diet.

Omega-3 (ALA) on the other hand is plant in high amounts in unctuous fish such as mackerel, salmon and tuna and may be slightly harder to obtain on an exclusively vegan or submissive baseddiet.However, try to include at least one-two portions of oily fish a week in your diet to ensure you are getting enough ALA, If you are just limiting your meatintake.However, similar as chia seeds, canola oil, If you are switching to an exclusively factory based diet be sure to include plenty of factory based sources of omega-3 per week.

Vegetables That Can Substitute for Meat

Tofu, Tempeh, Seitan, and TVP

You may not think of tofu or tempeh as vegetables, but they are plant-based and made from soybeans. TVP, or texturized vegetable protein, is also made from soy. Seitan is made from wheat gluten. The meat in any form can be replaced with one of these plant-based options. Tofu makes the perfect swap-out for chicken whether you want Crisp Tofu Nuggets, Moroccan Cutlets in a Lemon-Olive Sauce, or gobbets for Chinese food like Kung Pao Tofu. Tempeh is wonderful for fish dishes because it has a short texture. Try it in " Crab" Galettes or to make Breaded " Fish" Fillets. It can also be ground up to act as ground beef for Tempeh Meatballs or tacos. TVP comes in all shapes and sizes and it can replace any meat including ground beef. Try it in this Chik 'n Salad with Cranberries and Pistachios or in Tacos Sin Carne. Seitan can be seasoned to taste exactly like beef or pork. You wo n't believe the decadence you will get in a plate of Balsamic BBQ Seitan Ribs or a thick, juicy Seitan Steak in Beurre Blanc Sauce.

Mushrooms

When you want that meaty taste, that umami, mushrooms are the way to go. Their flavor is rich, earthy, and meaty, especially cremini or Portobello mushrooms. They are healthy and filling and can replace meat in any recipe. My favorite way to eat mushrooms is to saute them in vegan adulation and add thyme, black pepper, and balsamic vinegar. Then I serve them over polenta unless I 'm piling them up on a crisp roll to make a French Dip sandwich. Try mushrooms in this Mushroom Stroganoff or as a vegan " Lamb" Burger. Impress your dinner guests by serving them Stuffed Mushrooms with Pecans and Portobello Wellington.

Jackfruit

Still, you need to go out and get some, If you have not

yet tried jackfruit. Technically, jackfruit is a fruit but incredibly, it can stand in for meat in savory dishes. You can buy it raw or formerly cut up in a can. Jackfruit has a veritably slight sweet taste but not so much that you can't use it to make a decadent, satisfying Philly Cheesesteak. Jackfruit is perfect for regale sandwiches, stir-fries, or any dish that uses beef, funk, or pork.

Eggplant

When anyone goes veg, eggplant is probably the first vegetable that comes to mind, but you can do so much further with it than just make parmigiana. Eggplant has a rich, meaty taste and it's veritablyversatile.However, try it in these Eggplant Burgers and you will change your mind, If you think you 're not a fan of eggplant. Other succulent ways to eat eggplant include Vegan Mozzarella-Stuffed Eggplant Meatballs, crispy Eggplant Fries with Marinara Dipping Sauce, and spiralized Eggplant Noodles.

Lentils

Lentils have always been a stage- heft for meat since the morning of veganism. Lentils are hearty and can replace ground beef easily. Lentils come in a variety of colors such as green, red, brown, and black. They chef up quickly, are inexpensive, and a small quantum goes a long way. Definite fashions to try are Red Lentil Burgers with Kale Pesto, Lentil Meatballs, Double Decker Lentil Tacos, and South Indian Lentil Stew.

Sap and Legumes

Sap and legumes are amazing. They are inexpensive, healthy, filling, and there are so many to choose from black sap, order beans, pinto sap, aduki beans, chickpeas and black-eyed peas, to name just a few. Beans make for hearty mists, stews, and chilis. How about a White Bean and Kale Soup or a Tamale- Inspired Bowl with Sap? Beans and legumes can replace the meat to make incredible Hoisin Black Bean Burgers, Black-Eyed Pea Italian Bangers, or Chickpea " Tuna" Salad.

Cauliflower

Right now I bet you 're thinking, " How can cauliflower replace meat? It's so white and mellow." Well, it can. When you season it and cook it up right, cauliflower can be the star of any dish. I like to use cauliflower to replace the chicken in Asian dishes like Cauliflower Manchurian and even Buffalo bodies. You can slice the cauliflower into steaks and make an inconceivable Cauliflower Piccata. You can even make a pizza crust out of cauliflower. See? Cauliflower does n't feel so boring anymore, does it?

Potatoes

Potatoes are not just for side dishes. They can be the main component in so many dishes. Whether you roast them, boil them, bake them, mash them, or shindig them, potatoes are always a favorite. Start your meal with a Creamy Potato and Cauliflower Soup. Potato Samosas with Coconut-Mint Chutney are spicy and delicious. Add potatoes to your burgers like in this

Moussaka Burger with Béchamel Cheese Sauce and this Spicy Potato Cauliflower Burger. Do n't forget potatoes when it comes to cate – that's right. You will be blown away by this Chocolate Potato Cake.

Beets

Beets are nature's candy. They are sweet and succulent and perfect for salads, but they have another side to them. Beets are also earthy and work well in savory dishes especially when roasted as in this Sesame Roasted Beets and Greens Dish. Amaze your guests with a beautiful platter of Beet Carpaccio and then treat them to Roasted Beet Burgers with Cumin-Scented Ketchup. Finish the meal with Beetroot Chocolate Frosted Cupcakes.

Nuts

Ok, technically, nuts are not vegetables but they can be used to make vegan rubbish and to replace meat in your cuisine. Nuts can be incredibly " meaty" and can make a hearty and rich " meat" loaf for regale. Nuts are often added to vegan burgers for added " meatiness." Try these Kidney Bean – Walnut Burgers with Mississippi Comeback Sauce.

As you can see, when it comes to replacing meat in your refections, your options are practically limitless. Stop thinking of vegetables as side dishes and move them to the front of your plate. With all the hearty, " meaty" recipes you can create, there is no way you will miss the meat.

The plant-based diet is a order of diets that have this in common " All plant-based diets limit animal-derived foods in favor of plants," Yule says. Instead of a diet centered on meat and dairy, the starring roles are played by vegetables, fruit, and whole grains. It's a fresh, flavorful approach to eating and has been shown to have significant health benefits, including weight loss and complaint prevention.